Disaster Science

The Science of a Flood

MEG MARQUARDT

Published in the United States of America
by Cherry Lake Publishing
Ann Arbor, Michigan
www.cherrylakepublishing.com

Consultants: Stephen A. Nelson, Ph.D., Associate Professor of Earth and Environmental Sciences, Tulane University;
Marla Conn, ReadAbility, Inc.
Editorial direction: Red Line Editorial
Book production: Design Lab
Book design: Sleeping Bear Press

Photo Credits: Slobodan Miljevic/iStockphoto, cover, 1; Robert Ray/AP Images, 5; Charlie Neibergall/AP Images, 7;
iStockphoto, 9, 16; David J. Phillip/Pool/AP Images, 13; Bela Szandelszky/AP Images, 15; Daniel Teixeira/Agencia Estado/
AP Images, 18; Mark Humphrey/AP Images, 21; Dave Kolpack/AP Images, 24; Marit Hommedal/NTB/AP Images, 27;
Ron Bailey/iStockphoto, 28

Library of Congress Cataloging-in-Publication Data
 CIP data has been filed and is available at catalog.loc.gov.

Cherry Lake Publishing would like to acknowledge the work of
the Partnership for 21st Century Skills. Please visit www.p21.org
for more information.

Printed in the United States of America
Corporate Graphics
June 2015

ABOUT THE AUTHOR

Meg Marquardt was a scientist but decided she liked writing about science even more. She enjoys
researching physics, geology, and climate science. She lives in Omaha, Nebraska, with her two cats,
Lagrange and Doppler.

TABLE OF CONTENTS

THE MISSOURI RIVER FLOOD

In June 2011, the small town of Hamburg, Iowa, prepared for disaster. For months, heavy snow and rain had raised water levels in the nearby Missouri River. **Levees** helped protect the town from flooding. But on June 13, the force of the water created a large hole in a nearby levee. Floodwaters poured through the hole, destroying crops on farms close to the town. Days later, another levee broke. Water flowed onto fields, nearing Hamburg.

Officials needed to act quickly to prevent more damage. The town of 1,200 people was in danger. Experts predicted that flood levels could be up to 10 feet (3 m) high. The water levels would be high enough to destroy cars, homes, and other buildings. The flood was likely to cause deaths and injuries. Officials set up shelters away from the flood and **evacuated** people from their homes to help them stay safe. But they could not fix the levees on their own. They needed help to save the town.

When the Missouri River flooded, water covered roads and farms in Hamburg, Iowa.

Members of the Iowa National Guard and the US
Army Corps of Engineers (USACE) arrived to build a
temporary levee. Soldiers worked day and night driving
bulldozers and filling the levee with bags of sand.

Hamburg was not the only town coping with floods.
Many other towns and cities along the Missouri River
were also flooded. Record amounts of precipitation had
raised water levels. The previous winter had been very
snowy. Temperatures were colder than usual, so the

FLOOD PROTECTION USING LEVEES

Levees are large mounds of material along riverbanks that keep
water from spilling out. Some rivers have natural levees made of dirt.
Others have manmade levees made from mixtures of dirt, concrete,
sand, and steel. Levees play a major role in flood defense. Nearly half
of the US population lives in counties with levees. Though a levee
can help prevent floods, it can also be breached, or broken. High or
strong floodwaters sometimes cause levees to break.

Workers prepared sandbags to prevent further flooding in Hamburg.

snow took longer to melt. In some areas, it piled up. In the spring, the ice and snow finally began to thaw. The river overflowed with water. Then the rains came. Above-average rainfall added to the already bursting river. The resulting floods damaged many homes and businesses. In some places, the floodwaters did not **recede** for more than a month.

In Hamburg, the flood caused local businesses to close for months. Houses were damaged or destroyed. The emergency levee cost millions of dollars to

THE COST OF FLOODS

Floods can cause expensive damages to cities and towns. The cost of the Missouri River flood totaled $3.4 billion. Each year, floods in the United States cause an average of $7.8 billion in damages. Flood costs include building repairs as well as emergency supplies, such as sandbags and temporary shelters.

construct. But it stopped more water from flooding in. The floodwater eventually **dissipated**, and residents returned to their homes. Over time, they worked to repair houses, buildings, and streets.

Many other towns and cities have faced similar problems. Floods are the most common type of natural disaster in the United States. Some places are more prone to floods than others. However, floods can occur anywhere that rain or snow falls. Moving water has the power to carry off trees, cars, and even houses.

Floods can also damage crops and cause food shortages. Worldwide, floods affect an estimated 97 million people each year.

Scientists have developed computer models to **forecast** floods. Many communities have warning systems to alert residents about flood risks. People can also take steps to stay safe.

When floods occur, some homeowners use sandbags to construct flood barriers.

WHAT CAUSES FLOODS?

In the Hamburg flood, melted snow and rain raised water levels in the river. After the levees broke, the river overflowed onto dry land. This is known as an overspill. However, river or creek overspill is just one cause of flooding. Oceans can cause floods during strong storms. The melting of ice can also cause floods. Some floods occur far from bodies of water.

In heavy rain, a **flash flood** can strike almost anywhere with little or no warning. Flash floods usually happen within six hours of heavy rain. They can also occur within minutes of a dam or levee break. Urban areas are at high risk for flash floods. Cities often have few grassy spaces. The streets and sidewalks are made of concrete and asphalt. These materials do not absorb water like soil does. During heavy rain, urban water **runoff** can rapidly fill up sewer systems. As a result, streets start to flood.

HOW A FLASH FLOOD FORMS

When a flash flood happens, heavy rain falls onto saturated soil. In some areas, the rainfall runs down to a river or other body of water. The water level rises, flooding nearby land.

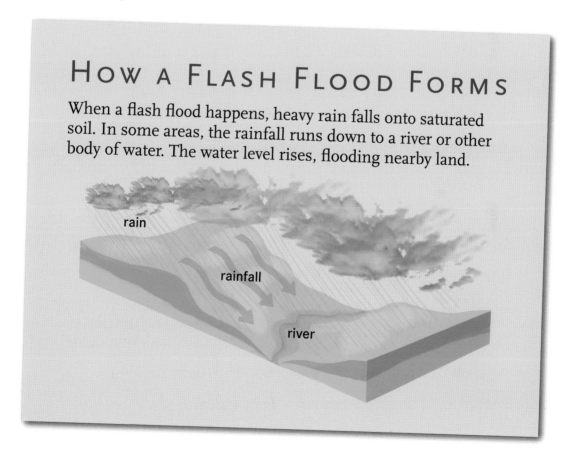

rain

rainfall

river

Flash floods are the number one cause of weather-related deaths in the United States. During flash floods, deaths and injuries most often occur when people drive cars in flooded areas. The water can carry away cars and cause accidents. If the water is deep enough, cars can sink.

During a large storm, such as a hurricane, winds drive water toward shorelines, causing it to pool up. The sea level rises. Sometimes the waves and wind push the water onto shore. This is known as a storm surge. The powerful waves can destroy buildings. Hurricane Katrina, one of the most destructive hurricanes in

SOIL SATURATION

Soil can soak up the moisture from rain and melted snow. However, the ground can hold only a certain amount of moisture. When it cannot hold more water, the soil is considered saturated. Saturated soil can worsen the impact of heavy rains, especially in the case of flash floods. Frozen ground can also prevent water from seeping into the soil.

*Two weeks after Hurricane Katrina hit
New Orleans, floods covered much of the city.*

American history, hit Louisiana in 2005. During the
hurricane, storm surges in New Orleans, Louisiana's
largest city, reached 10 to 18 feet (3 to 5 m). Due to
poorly constructed levees, floods covered approximately
80 percent of the city.

Even after a storm ends, floodwater may remain for
weeks or months. The duration of a flood often depends
on the area. Grassy areas may absorb water quickly. But
on low or saturated land, floodwater may have nowhere
to go. As a result, it can take a long time to dissipate.

THE DANGERS OF FLOODS

Minor floods during rainstorms are common, and few cause serious problems. However, severe floods may cause injuries, deaths, and property damage. They also create other problems. Floodwaters can **contaminate** groundwater, introducing dangerous chemicals into the water supply. Contaminated water can increase the risk of **communicable diseases**.

Most drinking water in the United States comes from groundwater wells. Rainwater is normally filtered as it moves through the ground. The soil strips away dangerous elements such as pollution or disease-causing bacteria. But if the soil is fully saturated with floodwater, the ground is not as effective at removing these dangers.

Floodwater can spread two types of communicable diseases. Water-borne illnesses, such as cholera, thrive in floodwater. When floodwaters enter a community's

In 2010, a scientist in Hungary tested water samples after a flood.

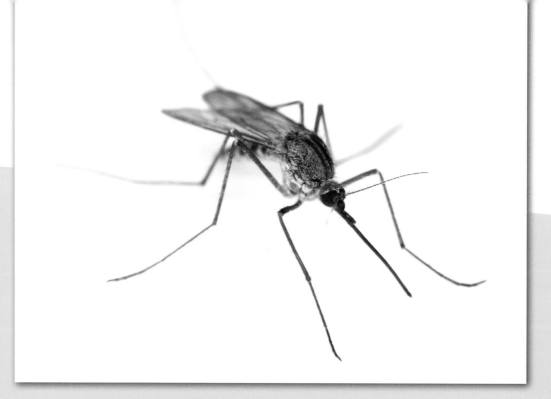

Mosquitoes thrive in flooded areas and can spread disease.

water supply, these illnesses can spread. Communities can prevent the spread of water-borne illnesses by providing clean water. Vector-borne diseases are spread by mosquitoes and other organisms. These diseases, such as malaria and the West Nile virus, can be harder to control. Floodwaters are prime breeding grounds for mosquitoes.

Floods also cause urban runoff. This runoff often contains bacteria and **pollutants** such as fertilizers, pesticides, and cleaning chemicals. These pollutants

16

can harm plants and animals. They increase people's risks of disease or infection. When they enter streams, they kill fish and other wildlife.

The threat of runoff near nuclear power plants is particularly dangerous. Floods around nuclear facilities can destroy equipment and release dangerous waste materials into cities or towns. Nuclear plants require a source of water to stay cool, so most are located near rivers, lakes, or oceans. However, these water sources increase the risk of flooding.

POSITIVE OUTCOMES OF FLOODING

Some floods have positive effects. Floodwaters move important elements, such as nutrients and sediments, that help make soil better for crops. They may also help a river or stream refresh its water source. This benefits the **ecosystem** of the river or stream.

As long as floodwater stays in an area, it can continue to cause problems. Even shallow water might contain dangerous pollutants. In hilly regions, floodwater often moves quickly. In flatter areas, floods usually move more slowly. This slow-moving water can create problems long after a storm has stopped.

In 2015, heavy rain caused flooding in the city of São Paulo, Brazil.

FLOODS DAMAGE OIL TANKS

In 2013, flooding along the South Platte River in Colorado reached oil wells. The pressure from the water knocked over crude oil storage tanks. More than 48,250 gallons (180,000 L) of oil leaked into floodwaters in north-central Colorado.

The leaks were a major concern. Oil spills can harm people, plants, and animals. Getting access to the damaged tanks proved difficult. The floodwaters were too high. Industry workers monitored the tanks and oil wells from the air. Where possible, trained workers entered sites to shut down the wells and clean up dangerous areas. Workers shut down other oil wells remotely, using equipment at another location. In all, 50 spills were reported. The worst site saw a spill of about 323 barrels of oil. That's an amount equivalent to 10,175 gallons (38,500 L).

PREDICTING FLOODS

Some floods are difficult to predict. But scientists have developed ways to anticipate floods. They can predict some floods months before they begin.

Flash floods develop quickly, with little or no warning. **Meteorologists** forecast these floods by observing how much water a location has recently received. In already swollen streams, any amount of heavy rain could cause a flash flood. Urban areas and places with saturated soil are also at risk of flash floods. When weather conditions are right for a storm, meteorologists study these areas closely.

[21ST CENTURY SKILLS LIBRARY]

Meteorologists at the National Weather Service monitor
weather conditions that could cause flooding.

If a storm has already started, meteorologists consider its speed and direction. If rain is falling very quickly, the storm is more likely to cause floods. Another factor is how quickly the storm is moving. A slow-moving thunderstorm is more likely to cause flooding than a fast one. This is because a slow-moving storm stays in one place for longer.

Scientists use records of past storms to predict the size, speed, and wind direction of future storms. They often create computer models of hypothetical, or imagined, storms to make their predictions.

FLOODS IN CHINA

Some places are especially prone to flooding. Many of the worst floods in history have occurred in China. Often, flooding in China happens along the Yellow River. This river has a large amount of silt, or mud. The mud sometimes clogs the river and causes it to overflow. Today, dams and levees help prevent flooding. But in past years, devastating floods affected the communities around the river.

One model is called Sea, Lake, and Overland Surges from Hurricanes (SLOSH). The National Weather Service created the model to learn more about how storm surges develop. SLOSH measures storm surge risk factors for different coastal regions. It helps scientists predict the height and strength of possible surges. Researchers use this information to determine how much destruction might occur during a particular surge. As a result, they can help communities prepare for floods.

Flooding often results from a combination of events. When a region has high levels of rain or snow over several months, water builds up in rivers and streams. Eventually, floods happen. **Hydrologists** regularly measure water levels in rivers, lakes, and streams. Meteorologists study weather patterns. These are weather events and conditions that tend to repeat over

FLOODPLAINS

Floodplains are low areas near rivers. They are subject to flooding when the river overflows past its banks, or borders. After a river reaches the bankfull stage, flooding begins.

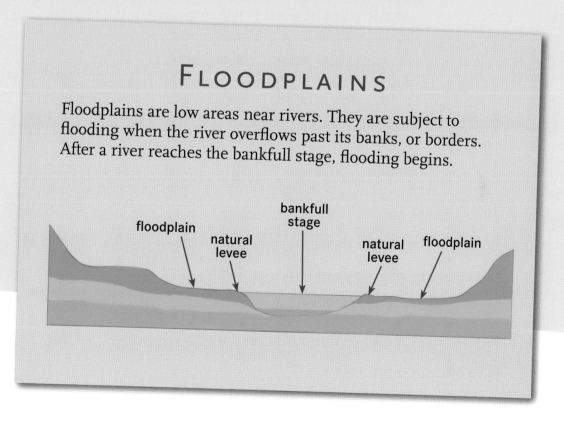

floodplain

natural levee

bankfull stage

natural levee

floodplain

Hydrologists with the US Geological Survey
prepare to take water measurements.

time. Some long-term weather patterns make floods more likely. Based on records of past years, meteorologists can estimate how much higher the water levels will rise. They can sometimes predict major floods months in advance.

Experts cannot predict every flood. Some flash floods develop unexpectedly. Several government agencies regularly collect information on flash floods. Scientists hope this data will continue to improve flood predictions.

SATELLITES THAT CAN PREDICT FLOODS

In 2002, NASA launched the Gravity Recovery and Climate Experiment (GRACE) satellites. Scientists designed the satellites to track changes in ice sheets on Earth. Later, they discovered that the satellites could also gather information about floods. GRACE satellites detect changes in mass on Earth's surface. When floods happen, the floodwater causes changes in mass in drainage basins. The satellites detect these changes and take detailed photographs of the areas. Scientists use the photographs to help measure water levels.

Researchers receive the GRACE photographs three months after they are taken. This delay limits the usefulness of the information. However, scientists are working to reduce the delay. Soon, they may be able to receive information only 15 days later. So far, scientists have used the GRACE satellites to study past flooding events. Soon, they hope to use the satellites to help them predict future floods.

CHAPTER 5

FLOOD PRECAUTIONS AND PREVENTION

Towns and cities use various methods to help prevent damage from floods. Levees help control water levels. Floodways can also affect water flow. A floodway is the land near a river channel. When the river overflows, it floods onto the floodway. Many communities limit construction on and near floodways. This prevents floods from reaching houses and other buildings.

Sometimes floods happen despite these precautions. When a flood is likely, meteorologists announce weather alerts. Knowing what to do before, during, and after a

In 2014, floods threatened homes in Norway.

flood is key to staying safe. Before a flood comes, people should gather useful items. Some people keep materials for building blockades. Homeowners can use sandbags to construct a barrier to keep out water.

If a flood is in progress, the best thing to do is seek higher ground. This could be an upper floor in a home or the top of a hill. People should not climb onto things that could be swept away, including cars. Community officials may evacuate an area if they think a flood will be severe.

Even after floodwaters dissipate, an area may not be completely safe. Floodwaters often weaken roads. Cracked roads can cause car accidents and injuries. If an area has been evacuated, people should wait for an all-clear alert before returning home. Once home, they should check for gas leaks. Some floods damage gas lines, which can cause explosions or illnesses.

A 2009 flood near Seattle, Washington, cracked and damaged roads.

HOW SCIENCE WORKS
FLOOD MAP SERVICE CENTER

The Federal Emergency Management Agency (FEMA) was created to help Americans recover from natural disasters. FEMA provides tools that people use to learn about flood threats in their area. One tool is the Flood Map Service Center, which provides maps of areas at risk for floods. FEMA officials work with scientists and local leaders to collect information about water levels, threatened areas, and recent weather events. They gather this information in each map. FEMA employees track possible changes to determine when new maps are needed.

People can use the maps to help prepare for possible floods. Some refer to the maps to make informed choices about where to buy or rent a home. Communities refer to the maps to improve emergency resources in their area.

Floods are common events in the United States and around the world. Having an emergency plan can help people and communities prepare for these disasters. As scientists develop new flood prediction tools, people's ability to prepare for floods will improve.

TOP FIVE WORST FLOODS

1. **1931: Yellow River, China**
   The Yellow River is about 3,000 miles (4,800 km) long. Large amounts of mud and silt in this river often cause it to overflow and flood. In 1931, floods lasted from July to November. Nearly four million people died in the floods.

2. **1887: Yellow River, China**
   Floods overran the dikes, or long walls, built around the Yellow River. Hundreds of thousands of people died. Diseases spread by the floodwaters raised the number of deaths to about two million.

3. **1938: Yellow River, China**
   During a war with Japan, Chinese forces destroyed levees around the Yellow River to slow the invading army. Water rapidly flowed out of the river, killing nearly 700,000 people.

4. **1975: Banqiao Dam Failure, China**
   Large amounts of rainfall caused the Banqiao Dam to collapse. Runoff created a wave that was 6.2 miles (10 km) wide. The massive wave surged into towns, causing the deaths of 171,000 people.

5. **1935: Yangtze River, China**
   Heavy rains caused floods along the longest river in Asia. The floodwaters destroyed crops, causing a famine. Nearly 145,000 people died due to the floods and famine.

LEARN MORE

FURTHER READING

Dougherty, Terri. *Anatomy of a Flood*. Mankato, MN: Capstone Press, 2011.

Markovics, Joyce. *Saving Animals after Floods*. New York, NY: Bearport Publishing Company, 2011.

Meyer, Susan. *Adapting to Flooding and Rising Sea Levels*. New York, NY: Rosen Publishing Group, 2012.

WEB SITES

Floods iQuest
http://pmm.nasa.gov/education/interactive/floods-iquest
This Web site provides lessons and activities about the causes and effects of flooding.

Ready: Floods
http://www.ready.gov/floods
This Web site offers useful information to help people prepare for floods.

GLOSSARY

communicable diseases (kuh-MYOO-ni-cah-bul diz-EEZ-ez) illnesses that can pass one organism to another, such as from a mosquito to a person

contaminate (kun-TAH-mi-nayt) make dirty or unsafe

dissipated (DISS-i-payt-ed) spread out and eventually disappeared

ecosystem (EE-coh-sis-tim) the community of plants and animals in a certain area

evacuated (EE-vak-you-ayt-ed) ordered to leave a dangerous place

flash flood (FLASH FLUD) a short local flood that may develop quickly

forecast (FOR-kast) predict when a certain event may occur

hydrologists (hi-DRAH-loh-jists) people who study the flow of water over Earth

levees (LEH-veez) natural or artificial barriers that prevent waterways from flooding

meteorologists (MEE-tee-or-ah-low-jists) people who predict and report on the weather

pollutants (puh-LOO-tunts) substances that make water or air unsafe

recede (ree-SEED) move back

runoff (RUHN-off) the flow of rain or other water on Earth's surface during storms

INDEX

[21ST CENTURY SKILLS LIBRARY]